My Everything Beautiful

Sean Michael LaValley

MY EVERYTHING BEAUTIFUL

SEAN MICHAEL LAVALLEY

COPYRIGHT © 2009 BY SEAN MICHAEL LAVALLEY.
ALL RIGHTS RESERVED.
No part of this book may be used or reproduced in any manner whatsoever without written permission by the author.

This book is a work of fiction produced by the author. Any names, characters, locations, and occurrences, are strictly fiction and of the author's imagination. Any similarities to actual persons, alive, or deceased, occurrences, and locations are exclusively coincidental .

ISBN 978-0-615-32347-3

for Grace Ann

I'll be your brightest midnight

If you'd be my shining star

Warm and inviting

I shall lie down

And surrender to you my horizon

And all else I hold beautiful

I will lend to you

My most favorite miracles

And watch you watch them

As I watch you

In immaculate amazement

Candles in bloom

Illuminating thunder

And all avenues of lavender temptation

Elegant and so addictive

The nature of your eloquent seduction

And in the mystery of evening

I propose eternity to you

And we melt like desert flowers

Together in the summer sun

I am reaching through decades for you

And I dream only of you

Always and only of you

There are small moments in time

Where all miracles come to life

And each tiny miracle is held

Beautifully behind brown eyes

Reach for me, again, I've fallen

I may be alive for a moment or two

Buried inside my soul is the sunshine

The light that I trust will carry me through

Free falling to the rhythm

Of her hypnotic symphony

The illusion of my sweetest memory

Now presenting in dimensional preciseness

Be beautiful always

Desire my truth

And bury me awake and with you

In choosing to render my heart helpless

I unfold my lavender wings

And wrap them warm around you

For as long as I can breathe with open arms

May all my dreams be always and only of you

Let me fall from thy grace

In hope I shall see you smile

Let me bury my fears in trust

That I can suffer my tears

Within your deepest ocean

And alone, be born

To your brightest dawn

Where I may weep

Unbridled to your sweetest sunrise

In the absence of light

I beckon the sound

Of your silent and most sincere color

I want to taste blindly

The shapes of all miracles

Held safely behind your ever burning beauty

Smoking my mind

To your sweetest reflection

For the sound of your dreaming

Has risen my sun

Fallen numb to your drumming

Compulsive and elusive enchantment

Burning blue for your freedom

I melt myself away in the rain

And I'm still here, awkward and enlightened

With lips that pray to someday know your name

In the company of memories

I summon thee, though dreaming

Blindly and contently, to the cortex

Of my conscious and hideous delusion

I remedy all ailments

And bury the lament of my wanting

In the coherence of my imaginary reality

I shall love you always

Through midnight enthralled

I seek still my truth in you

Lover, awake

The sun is growing warm upon you

And my body and mind are craving you

And your tepid rhythm

Immaculate resonation

Webbed inside of her heartbeat

To create is to understand

And with eyes, jeweled with compassion

The sky stands no chance at darkness

Thieves in search of riches

Explore the sea for gold

For I hold true, my treasure

She's the one I'd die to hold

To kiss her is to live again

For this, the Earth I've sold

To love her is to breathe again

As all my dreams unfold

Bleeding the jewel

The holiest of roses

And kissing the dawn

Of thy golden-haired goddess

I'm drunk off the nectar

That her body produces

And we welcome the silence

Of our unbreakable breathing

Weeping softly, still aware

My sleep land scented by her hair

Awake and shaking, how intriguing

That my body still somehow is breathing

Caught inside a moonlight high

Tripping on stars and sipping on sky

Dancing close, just she and I

In hope this night will never die

Her heart tucked warm inside of mine

We fuck, we drunk on sweat and wine

All of our hours exist

On an extravagant continuum

A supernatural heartbeat

That quietly dances

To the beating rhythm

Of its own pulse

Sometimes, although exhausted,

I lie awake and meditate

To the rhythm of your breathing

There exists evidence of subliminal isolation

Mindful illusion of self degradation

Sought after to heal my primary purpose

Believe in me and make me real

Bountiful and beautiful so

This heart is engraved with your name

And whispers your silent reflection

Touch and awaken

And allow me to travel

The depths of your consciousness

Grant me the moment to taste

Your most sensual secret

And relive this moment, over and over

For the rest of our lives

Can you slowly, breathing deeply

Shelter me inside your eyes

From you my dear, I dare not hide

Speaking softly, glowing holy

Glory we in sweet surprise

She now dancing by my side

My darling by my side

My soul one by my side

Falling through years of an unreserved beauty

I kiss cool the sky that once made her weep

The stars they keep falling

But there's one star I'm dreaming

And if it falls through me

That one star, I'll keep

In thy darkest hour

I melt through years of thunder

Begging for your heartbeat

I breathe beneath my wonder

And in the brightest moment

I summon sweet sensation

I fall to dreams of you

And burn through my elation

Brilliant and bright

In the magic of night

I dream of her flesh

So warm and snow white

Not near, nor she far

That diamond, that star

I'm breathing and dreaming

Of her, bathed in my light

I.

I've swallowed tiny pills

That looked just like your sky

I awoke in unknown cities

With wings that couldn't fly

I crawled a thousand miles

On littered streets of glass

And marveled at your kingdom

That I had found, at last

II.

Your gate was numb and lonely

I begged to be let in

For years there was no answer

I begged, and begged again

III.

My hope was growing tired

A beard adorned my face

And I swore if you didn't answer

I'd die beside your gate

IV.

One day I awoke from darkness

To the sound of the opening gate

For now I knew the lifetime here

Was worth the lengthy wait…

But then a figure stood before me,

A man with a mask and a sword

He raised his arm in the moonlight

"I've been ordered by my lord"

V.

His blade, it rushed through the moonbeams

Then I watched the figure fall

For the queen I've waited my life for

Was behind him standing tall

A pistol smoked in her left hand

A candle burned in her right

She more beautiful than ever

Had saved my life that night

Lover, awake

The stars have fallen from your eyes while sleeping

And your fertile garden grew shadows

In the absence of your ghosts

Your sky alive with wonder,

And your body warm from dreaming

Lover, awake

And behold my miracles, with me

Touch and be taken

To a kingdom I know

Where the tears of our angels

Fall upon us as snow

The moon and her envy

Kiss your eyes with their glow

And I'm falling through winter

And through you, as you know

In the end

The garden is still yours

And the energy is still summoned for only you

The words and dreams I live by are for you

All I've ever wanted was you

All that you are, is the perfection that I adore

When you fall, I shall catch you

When you cry, I shall cry with you

When you cannot breathe, I will breathe for you

When you cannot feel, I shall protect you

And in harmony with you, I would open my heart

And expose to you the essence of all that you are

And all the things I love, so very much about you

I will give my everything for you

And in the end, I will always love you

No matter how far away I am from you

I seek the dark

To trust the light

From the star

That gave me sight

I dream awake

Of visions true

In hope these dreams

Will bring me you

I love to hear you say

"I love you"

In your presence

I am so aware

Conscious of what I want

You, only you

I am no one until you awaken

Sleep through me, love

Your kiss permeates me

With seductive intention

A solemn sequence

Of proverbial promise

Your mouth on fire with mine

Your body warm and wet

Inviting me slow inside

We taste together

And witness new awakenings

Tiptoe on this warming rainbow

That I have created from all the joy

Inside of my beating heart

My most brutal and insane desires

Paint these unknown colors for you

To taste, and to awaken to

In fields of purple clover

Rest my body soft in the land

Kiss me to sleep and wish my eyes

Safe passage to my serenity

Your body is like velvet

Warm with sweat and perfume…

I am the thunder and she is my sky

She is the whisper that lent me my dreams

Together we create symphonies, grand orchestras

That ring silent on the ears of all strangers

Star so light and oh so bright

Guide me through your veins tonight

Tickle touch, and yield a trust

To live a life that fuels our lust

Years awake and without light

I bleed the need to summon sight

To witness pride, as once had I

As I have you, right by my side

Destined we, one

Naked, though clothed

By the warm summer sun

The softest endeavor

Gloried in truth

Bathed in forever, together

Warm be you and strong by me

Sip soft the sky and taste slow the sea

Your beauty has beckoned the best out of me

And I have so fallen in love deep with thee

Smile, my love sweetly

How you melt my world away

And with your eyes of light, my love

Night skies turn to day

My truth, my love, is endless

And our sun, my love, burns bright

With you, my love, I am in love

And this love with you feels right

In the sands of eternity

I scribble slowly the sanctity of your name

Finding sanctuary and warm surprise

When wrapped in the warmth of your wings

Your body, beautifully moving

To the rhythm of our sacred dance

Spilling secrets, from deep

I swallow you in your most erotic instance

And we elevate together, in warm eruption

Toward our everlasting eternity

And the angel said…

"I don't think she should throw away her halo

But instead, embrace it."

www.ingramcontent.com/pod-product-compliance
Lightning Source LLC
Chambersburg PA
CBHW031217090426
42736CB00009B/961